CANALS
IN THE HEART OF
ENGLAND

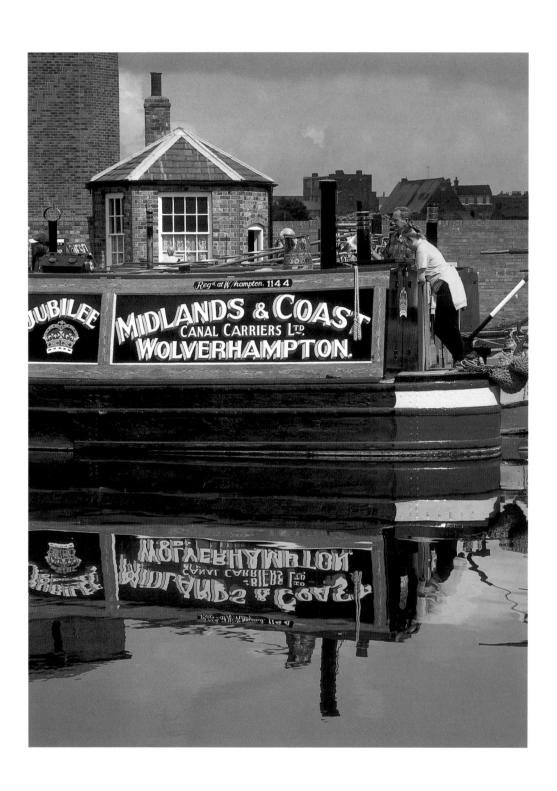

CANALS
IN THE HEART OF
ENGLAND

ALAN TYERS

BREWIN BOOKS

Published by Brewin Books Ltd
Studley, Warwickshire B80 7LG
in 2002

www.brewinbooks.com

ISBN 1 85858 212 1

British Library Cataloguing in Publication Data
A Catalogue record for this book is available from the British Library.

Printed by Heron Press, Kings Norton, Birmingham.

Frontispiece: Beautifully restored working boat Jubilee at Cambrian Wharf, Birmingham, during the weekend of the first Inland Waterways Exhibition, held at the National Indoor Arena.

In the background is the restored Toll Office that marks the start of the Birmingham and Fazeley Canal. Deep in conversation are Lucie Hancock of British Waterways, Fradley and Fred Heritage an original boater and working boat volunteer.

CONTENTS

INTRODUCTION

Britain's canals have dramatically changed over the last decade and their renaissance from a run-down, abandoned, vandalised and underused system to a major national asset is largely down to British Waterways and forward thinking local authorities. Of the 2000 miles of waterway British Waterways own and manage, the Heart of England network has provided me with a rich seam of subject matter, both through commissions from British Waterways and personal projects.

This photographic essay covers several of the canals that navigate through the Heart of England.

They say there are more miles of canals in Birmingham than Venice and many featured in this book begin in the Midlands.

Gas Street Basin and the area around the International Convention Centre, National Indoor Arena, and Brindleyplace, form a dramatic backdrop alongside the traditional design and architecture of the canal. The Birmingham and Fazeley begins at the junction by the NIA and travels under Spaghetti Junction via Kingsbury to Fradley near Lichfield. The Birmingham and Worcester begins at Gas Street Basin and includes the famous Tardebigge flight. The Stratford-upon-Avon canal runs from Bancroft Gardens in the centre of the town via Kingswood Junction at Lapworth, where the Grand Union begins, and includes three famous aqueducts. Knowle locks and Hatton have also provided wonderful locations on the Grand Union. A Russell Newbury Rally took me to the Black Country Museum on the Dudley Canal. Closer to home, I found myself on the '5½', the boaters popular name for the 5½ mile section of the Coventry Canal from the city centre basin to Hawkesbury Junction. Finally, starting at Hawkesbury, the Oxford Canal has provided some wonderful rural locations.

Along the way I have enjoyed meeting and photographing boaters, British Waterways personnel, and skilled craftsmen and women who are carrying on the great traditions of canal crafts, and who all share a common interest in the regeneration of the canals of the Heart of England.

But what draws me time and again is the visual atmosphere that only English canals have, whether in an urban or rural environment, through the design, style and detail of the architecture of its buildings, bridges and locks, and the shapes and graphics of the narrow boats with their lettering and pictures. Add to this the occasional lucky break with a particular weather effect or a person appearing right on cue and you have the essence of a picture that captures the mood of the scene. I hope therefore the following personal images inspire you to visit and explore canals in your region and enjoy them.

As a photographer I've always supported the old adage that 'one picture is worth a thousand words', so the prospect of writing all the captions was fairly daunting. However, once I'd got into it I found that researching the history and finding out more about the canals became quite fascinating, so I hope they add interest to the photographs. As I'm no historian or expert I've relied on a number of reference sources for historical accuracy, plus talking to people about particular canals, as well as including my own personal views, both in words and pictures.

CHAPTER ONE

COVENTRY CANAL

Sculpture by Reg Butler RA of James Brindley, the renowned engineer and surveyor who was elected by the committee of promoters for the Coventry Canal, after the Act of Parliament received the Royal Assent on 29 January 1768. The first sod was cut in Foleshill in May of the same year.

COVENTRY CANAL

The statue of James Brindley is located in the canal basin in Coventry City Centre and marks the beginning of Britain's longest outdoor gallery. The bronze is over life size and depicts Brindley studying a drawing of bridge No.1 that he designed and built.

There are 39 artworks by 31 artists located along the '5½' from Coventry Canal basin to Hawkesbury Junction.

The Coventry Canal Company's terminal wharf, known as Coventry Basin, was opened to traffic in August 1769. Situated in an area known as Bishopgate after one of the city's gates, it features the distinctive row of warehouses which back onto Leicester Row, with their canopies and hoists now restored to their former glory. But the basin no longer echoes to the sound of grain sacks from London being off loaded from horse drawn boats and hoisted into waiting vans to be taken to the local flour mills.

Peter Freakley making rope fenders at a Traditional Canal Craft Fair held in Coventry Basin. Although a boater for 45 years Peter no longer owns a boat, but attends many events demonstrating this art which dates back generations.

Model, Fellows, Morton & Clayton narrowboat at a Traditional Waterways Fair in Coventry Basin. Fellows, Morton & Clayton were one of the main commercial carriers who operated in the heyday of the canals. Based in Birmingham, as well as a considerable fleet of boats, horse drawn carts, wagons and steam lorries, they also owned and built several warehouses, particularly Sherborne Street Wharf, and Crescent Wharf on the Newhall Branch of the Birmingham and Fazeley Canal, which became known as Cambrian Wharf. They also had warehouses on the Warwick and Birmingham at Fazeley Wharf and the Old and New Warwick Wharfs on the Digbeth Branch.

The traditional art of canal ware painting, commonly called 'Roses and Castles', is still practised by a number of artists, including Trevor Hail, seen here demonstrating at a British Waterways Craft Fair in Coventry Basin.

The exact construction date of the warehouses is not known, but a map dated 1837 includes them, however they appear to be much older than this date. There is also evidence that some rebuilding has taken place from the first floor upwards at the Bishop Street end as some of the rooms have iron pillars with the date 1914 cast into them.

Although no longer in working order, the crane used for loading and unloading the boats moored in the central area has been restored and retained as a reminder of the historical past of the basin.

COVENTRY CANAL

The Coventry Canal is 38 miles long and ends at Fradley Junction near Lichfield. The section between Coventry and Hawkesbury Junction on the outskirts of Coventry and Bedworth is known as the '5½' by boaters. Originally built to transport coal from the mines in the Bedworth and Nuneaton area, it joins the Oxford Canal at Hawkesbury. A quarter of a mile away on the Oxford at Tusses Bridge was the Longford power station, known locally as 'Coventry Light'. James Brindley also engineered the Oxford Canal.

COVENTRY CANAL

In 1983 development proposals for the basin were actioned to regenerate the area and create a city amenity. Subsequent redevelopment in the 90's has seen the restoration of the old Leicester Row warehouse, new offices, shops and a tearoom built on the opposite side of the basin and the original coal vaults are now used as a restaurant. The distinctive warehouse now houses a variety of businesses, including artists' studios, design groups and high tech companies. The central area now plays host to numerous events and fairs, which is breathing new life back into Coventry Basin.

Looking towards Coventry City Centre from bridge No. 2, Cash's Lane. In the distance can be seen the famous three spires of St. Michaels Cathedral, Holy Trinity Church, and Christchurch.

While photographing the previous view early one morning the gentleman above arrived and proceeded to feed a pair of swans which had been swimming around all the time I was there. He told me that he feeds the pair at Cash's lane and a pair at Coventry Basin every day of the year, including Christmas Day.

There is currently a major programme of wildlife conservation taking place along the '5½' to encourage wildlife back to their natural habitat, with sections of the bank having coir matting installed to encourage animals such as water voles, as well as plants and other animals.

COVENTRY CANAL

On the other side of Bridge No.2 that in the past was known as Honey Lane Bridge, is the historic landmark of Cash's Hundred House. Joseph Cash, who established the world famous company, J&J Cash, silk weavers, had these houses built in 1857. Originally only 48 were ever built and now only 37 remain, having been restored and converted into flats. The grade 1 listed building provided housing on the ground and first floors with the looms on the top floor. Because of this they were also known as 'Top Shops'.

COVENTRY CANAL

Hawkesbury, the famous junction of the Coventry Canal and Oxford Canal with its beautiful Britannia Bridge spanning the two basins. The bridge was cast at the foundry of John Sinclair, near Derby, who was engineer to the Coventry Canal Company from 1820-1863. It was installed in 1837 when he made improvements and the two canals were joined at Hawkesbury. Prior to these improvements they joined at Longford, a mile south, and ran parallel to each other.

Under the bridge can be glimpsed the engine house which housed a Newcomen atmospheric engine of 1821,called Lady Godiva and a second engine, named The Earl of Mercia, which was installed in 1837. They cleared drained water from Exhall Colliery and Bedworth Field, pumping it from a well into the canal.

COVENTRY CANAL

A view under John Sinclair's Britannia Bridge, which spans the turn from the Coventry to the Oxford Canal. Looking south the Coventry Canal is on the right, the building in the centre is on the site of the Toll Office, which controlled the operation of the numerous boats that converged at Hawkesbury. The row of original cottages on the left ran down the lane to the railway bridge which spanned the lane and the Coventry Canal and was built by the LNWR to Wyken Alexandra and Wyken Old Main Pit collieries and the Power Station at Longford.

Looking back to the start of the Oxford Canal, with the roving bridge, stop lock and John Sinclair's Bridge in the distance. Hawkesbury Junction is also known as Sutton Stop or Suttons, after Richard Sutton (1769-1846) a local toll clerk who worked at the junction.

The narrow stop lock under the bridge was built to stop one canal emptying the water of the other. It was also where boats had to stop to be gauged and the appropriate toll paid.

The roving bridge is built to take the towpath from one side of the canal to the other, the round coping stones on the wall allowing the rope of the horse drawn boats to slide over easily.

CHAPTER TWO

STRATFORD-UPON-AVON CANAL

The Stratford-upon-Avon Canal joins the Upper Avon Navigation at Bancroft Gardens, which opens up the route from Birmingham to Tewkesbury and the River Severn. Travelling the short distance from the canal to the lock alongside the weir on the Avon, you pass the Royal Shakespeare Memorial Theatre and Holy Trinity Church, where William Shakespeare is buried. This access to the Avon is popular for narrow boat cruises as it forms part of the Warwickshire and Avon cruising rings.

STRATFORD-UPON-AVON CANAL

The entrance into the Stratford-upon-Avon canal from the River Avon. The narrow boats have come up the Upper Navigation and are entering the broad river lock 'two-handed', which means they are side-by-side, therefore saving time and water. The ever-present swans and ducks are a feature of this popular part of town. In fact, William Shakespeare is often referred to as the Swan of Avon.

The Act of Parliament for the construction of the Stratford-upon-Avon, from Kings Norton near Birmingham, where it joined the Worcester and Birmingham, to Stratford was passed in 1793. However, construction only reached Hockley Heath in 1796, when its funds ran out.

STRATFORD-UPON-AVON CANAL

The construction of the section of the Stratford-upon-Avon Canal from Hockley Heath to Kingswood Junction at Lapworth was completed in May 1802. Josiah Clowes and Samuel Porter engineered this northern section of the canal. For the next 10 years Kingswood remained the terminus until work started in 1812 to complete the southern section.

At the entrance to the canal from the River Avon is a bridge constructed in the style of the distinctive split bridges, which are a feature of this attractive canal. It is guarded over by a bronze statue of Adam.

STRATFORD-UPON-AVON CANAL

William Whitemore engineered the southern section of the Stratford-upon-Avon, from Kingswood Junction to Bancroft Gardens basin, between 1812-1816. It appears to have been built 'on the cheap' during the Napoleonic Wars and includes many unusual cost-cutting designs, as well as distinctive aqueducts.

The canal was also envisaged as part of a transport centre, conceived by William James, who owned the Upper Avon river, who built a tramway from Stratford towards Moreton-in-Marsh and who superintended the canal. The route of the tramway, together with a restored wagon and length of track, can be seen in front of the buildings, which are now Cox's Yard, seen in the distance.

Entering Bancroft Gardens basin via the wide river lock means passing under a bridge designed in the form of the split bridges on the Stratford-upon-Avon canal. This bridge was constructed by men from HM Prison Wormwood Scrubs and HM Prison Birmingham, at the time the canal was leased by The National Trust in the 1960's. Another interesting feature is the angled beam on the lock gates, which is due to the closeness of the bridge to the lock.

The southern section of the Stratford-upon-Avon Canal also has six distinctive lockkeepers cottages with unique barrel roofs, which were based on bridge construction techniques and thought to have been adopted to save money.

At the end of the canal at Bancroft in Stratford-upon-Avon there were originally 2 basins, including 11 coal wharves, one lead wharf, one glass wharf and one timber wharf. In 1903 however, one of the basins was filled in and Bancroft Gardens became the terminus.

Today it is a major focal point of the town, both for visitors and boaters, with moorings in the basin. There is also a youth club, an art gallery, ice cream and a sandwich boat permanently moored here, plus a luxury restaurant boat that operates from the basin.

I came across this man in Bancroft Gardens making rope fenders in the old traditional way. There are still a number of commercial makers and professional craftsmen practising the art, but this boater does it as a hobby and for relaxation.

Working alongside his narrow boat, moored in the basin, it's hard to think that this canal was almost abandoned and recommended for closure in 1955. When in 1846 it was purchased by the Oxford, Worcester and Wolverhampton Railway, later the GWR, it was progressively run down by them in favour of their rail transport. The final boat passed through the southern section in the 1920's. But its renaissance is an important part of post war canal restoration history, led by dedicated individuals like Tom Rolt and the Inland Waterways Association.

Thanks to public protest and the formation of the Stratford-upon-Avon Canal Society in 1956 work began to restore it to its former glory. In 1960 The National Trust obtained a lease on the waterway and restoration was continued. On 11 July 1964 the canal was re-opened by Queen Elizabeth the Queen Mother.

The Stratford-upon-Avon Canal has along the southern section 3 examples, of which there are only 6 in the country, of cast iron trough aqueducts. All three are grade II* listed buildings. All three were built between 1812-1816. Also along the 26 mile canal there are over 40 structures and buildings listed grade II, including 4 that are grade II*. These include twelve locks; twenty-one bridges, six lock side cottages, an engine house and the Lapworth office and workshop of British Waterways.

Of the three aqueducts on the Stratford-upon-Avon the longest is Edstone or Bearley, at 130 metres long. In fact it is the second longest aqueduct in the country. It was built in 1813 and crosses Salters Lane, a stream and the former GWR line from Birmingham Snow Hill to Stratford, as well as a field.

Edstone aqueduct is a mile from Bearley village and a mile north of Wilmcote village, the location of Mary Arden's House. One of its features, and of all the Stratford-upon-Avon Canal aqueducts is the towpath alongside the trough that is built with cast iron plates, wide enough for a 7-foot boat that carries the waterway.

Edstone aqueduct is by any standard impressive; as it dominates the small valley it crosses. It is supported on 14 brick piers with cast iron beams between each pier. During the canal's period of ownership by the GWR, Edstone aqueduct was used as a water tank for the engines. The original plug for draining via a pipe into the field below was sealed and a new outlet installed, which has also since been removed. Ironically, regular steam train services are again operating between Birmingham and Stratford during the summer, using restored GWR engines and coaches.

Wootten Wawen aqueduct crosses the busy A3400, Birmingham Road, 5 miles north of Stratford-upon-Avon. Completed in October 1813 it is classed as a scheduled monument. Similar to Edstone the cast iron water trough stands on 3 brick piers with cast iron beams. Two unusual features of the aqueduct are a cast iron mile marker at the south end, which is GWR in origin and a plaque on the Stratford side, which reads: The Stratford Canal Comp.y erected this aquaduct in October 1813. Bernard Dewes Esq. Chairman. W. James Esq. Dep.t Chairman. William Whitmore Engineer.

STRATFORD-UPON-AVON CANAL

At the northern end of Wootten Wawen aqueduct is a basin, which was originally built as a wharf to allow goods and materials to be transported for the final stretch of the construction to Stratford. In 1962 this wharf was taken over and is now the home of the Anglo Welsh Boat Hire Company. Next to the wharf is also the Navigation Inn, one of the many attractive canal side pubs to be discovered along the Stratford-upon-Avon canal. The distinctive gantry structure at the end of the aqueduct was erected in the 1970's by the boat hire company to lift engines in and out of boats. It is still in use today being used during the winter stoppage period between October and Easter.

STRATFORD-UPON-AVON CANAL

Yarningale aqueduct is located in the hamlet of Yarningale Common, close to a lock and one of the Stratford-upon-Avon's distinctive barrel roofed lock side cottages. Situated in a peaceful rural setting it crosses a stream. Originally it was built in 1813, but a plaque on the western side commemorates the installation of a new water trough by the Horsley Iron Company, the world leader of the day in iron castings, and dated 1834.

Maintaining and keeping the canal in good order is a year round task and represents a major behind-the-scenes operation many people do not see, particularly during the winter stoppage period.

At Wilmcote, Pete Chamberlain, lockkeeper at Wilmcote and Ian Trevor carry out hedgelaying on a bright winter morning. Due to a number of appearances on the television programme Waterworld, Pete Chamberlain - left, has become a recognised ambassador for canals in general and the Stratford-Upon-Avon in particular.

CHAPTER THREE

BIRMINGHAM CANAL NAVIGATIONS

The renaissance of Birmingham City Centre is a remarkable mixture of the old and the new and the area around Broad Street, centred around the canal network, has transformed the city in the 21st century beyond recognition.

It was 3 centuries earlier in 1769 that the first of the cities canals, from Wednesbury to Newhall and Gas Street, was engineered and built by James Brindley. Known as the Old Main Line it was extended to Wolverhampton in 1772. The route was further improved by Thomas Telford in the 1820's who built a more direct route, which became known as the New Main Line.

The view above, at Old Turn Junction or Deep Cutting Junction, is looking down the Old Main Line to Gas Street. The Horseley iron bridge crosses the Birmingham and Fazeley, which now begins at this junction.

Looking along the Old Main Line to Broad Street from the bridge that crossed the entrance to Brewery Basin. The malt houses and brewery of the Birmingham Brewery are now replaced with the boiler house of the International Convention Centre and National Indoor Arena.

Three centuries of history in the centre of Birmingham. The Old Main Line canal in the foreground is now dominated by the hugely successful ICC. Sandwiched between them is the sympathetically restored Brewery House of the old Birmingham Brewery.

Looking across from Brindleyplace and the Waters Edge development to the ICC. This whole area is now a lively, vibrant centre to rival any European city, and a far cry from the run-down forgotten amenity that Birmingham's canals had become in the 1970's and 80's.

Around the area are a number of artworks, including a plaque on the wall of the ICC to James Brindley, the engineer who began it all back in 1769.

Paris? Amsterdam?

The canal network in Birmingham is now a major part of the city's tourist attractions. There are now a number of trip boats that take visitors along the canals, but this is not a new feature of the Birmingham Canal Navigations.

Passenger boats, originally known as packet boats, travelled both the Old and New Main Lines as early as 1800. However they had ceased operating by 1852.

One of the features of the Old Main Line before restoration were the high walls of factories that hid the canal from view. Looking across to the ICC and Hyatt International these walls have now become an attractive architectural feature of the area. Beyond the wall can be seen the Crown Public House, a listed building which faced onto what was St. Peter's Place.

To the right the original buildings on Broad Street have been restored and now house restaurants and bars.

The narrow boat is approaching Broad Street tunnel, with a glimpse of Gas Street Basin in the distance.

Looking across Gas Street Basin from the pedestrian entrance of Gas Street itself. This is the junction between the Birmingham Canal Navigation Old Main Line and the Worcester and Birmingham Canal and is the centre of the Broad Street area. The footbridge, which is not an original feature but was the first cast iron bridge to be made for 150 years using the original Horseley Iron Works designs, was installed during the improvements of the early 1990's. It gives access to the basins moorings and spans the original 7 foot transhipment jetty, known as Worcester Bar.

Restored working and residential boats moored in Gas Street Basin, with their traditional lettering and decorated canal ware. Ash was owned by the Birmingham & Midland Canal Carrying Company, one of a number of carriers, including Fellows, Morton and Clayton, who also operated from Birmingham.

The tall brick buildings in the background were originally a grain warehouse, cottages and the Birmingham Canal Company's lock cottage. In the distance, towering above the buildings of Broad Street is the Italianate tower that is part of the Brindleyplace development.

One of the pleasures of the revitalised canals of Birmingham is the opportunity to just sit, have a meal or drink and watch the world go by, on foot, or on a boat. The bay window in the foreground is part of the Worcester & Birmingham Canal Toll office, which was constructed in 1893 and which replaced an earlier one.

One of the many trip boats on the Birmingham Canal Navigation approaches Worcester Bar. Originally the canal stopped where the new bridge spans the canal because the companies jealously guarded their water. However, in 1815 the BCN Company came to an agreement with the Worcester & Birmingham and the bar was pierced by a stop lock. Today that has been removed allowing an uninterrupted passage.

CHAPTER FOUR

BIRMINGHAM & FAZELEY CANAL

The Birmingham & Fazeley Canal begins at the Old Turn Junction and joins the Coventry Canal at Fazeley, 15 miles away. Moored outside the National Indoor Arena at the first Inland Waterways Exhibition is the preserved working boat President.

Originally belonging to Fellows, Morton & Clayton, President is the only working steam-powered narrow boat now in existence. Purchased by a group of enthusiasts in 1973 it was restored to its original 1909 condition in 1978. Fellows originally had over 30 steamers for fly or express working between Birmingham and London or the East Midlands and London.

BIRMINGHAM & FAZELEY CANAL

The Birmingham and Fazeley was engineered by John Smeaton and opened in 1789. A group of working boats assembled in the length between Old Turn Junction and Tindal Bridge recreate a scene from yesteryear. The boatman, dressed in traditional clothes of the period, beats a rug on the stern of his boat. To the left is President and behind are the old Kingston Buildings. These were used in the early 1800's as a nail and metal warehouse. Now called Austin Court they are a conference and lecture centre.

A view looking towards Tindal Bridge from Cambrian Wharf.

This area became known as Farmer's Bridge when in 1769, when the Newhall Branch was completed, an accommodation bridge was built for the landowner and Birmingham gunmaker, James Farmer. The original bridge was located behind the white cottage on the right to the white cottage on the left and was taken down during the 1820's when the canal was widened. The cottages on the left are known as Kingston Row and still carry the canal company's property number plates.

BIRMINGHAM & FAZELEY CANAL

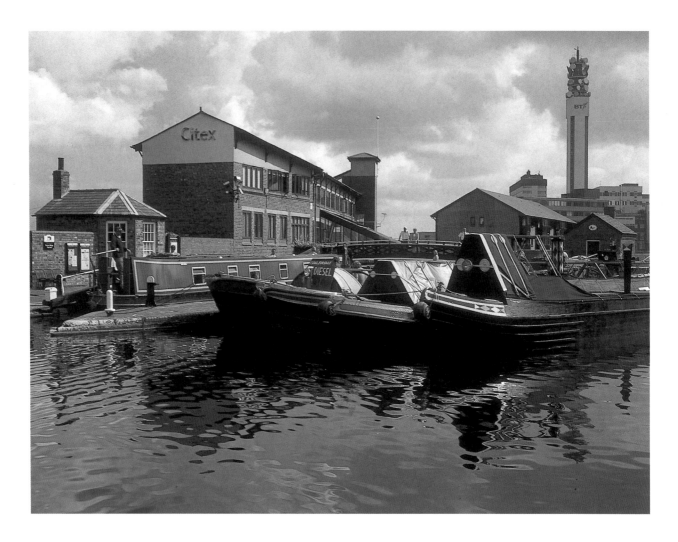

The old Farmer's Bridge Junction, now known as Cambrian Wharf, which was originally the Newhall Branch and terminus of the Birmingham Canal in 1772.

This branch and Crescent Wharf became an important carrier depot with a number of warehouses and which several independent canal-carrying companies owned.

The boat on the left is entering the top lock at the start of the Farmer's Bridge Flight. Moored in the wharf are a number of working boats gathered for the Inland Waterways Exhibition. In the distance is the BT Tower, Birmingham's tallest building, which straddles the Birmingham & Fazeley Canal.

The beginning of the Farmer's Bridge Flight, known as The Old Thirteen, looking back to the NIA with Cambrian Wharf on the left. Already the canal has dropped significantly and continues on to Lock 13, a total drop of 81 feet, which is located beneath the viaduct of the former GWR line from Snow Hill Station.

The restored toll office that stands alongside the top lock marked the start of the Birmingham & Fazeley Canal. Here boats were gauged with sticks to measure the draft of the boat and tolls charged accordingly.

Although the scene is now dominated by the National Indoor Arena the redevelopment of this area and the restoration of the canal now provides a very attractive leisure amenity right in the heart of Birmingham.

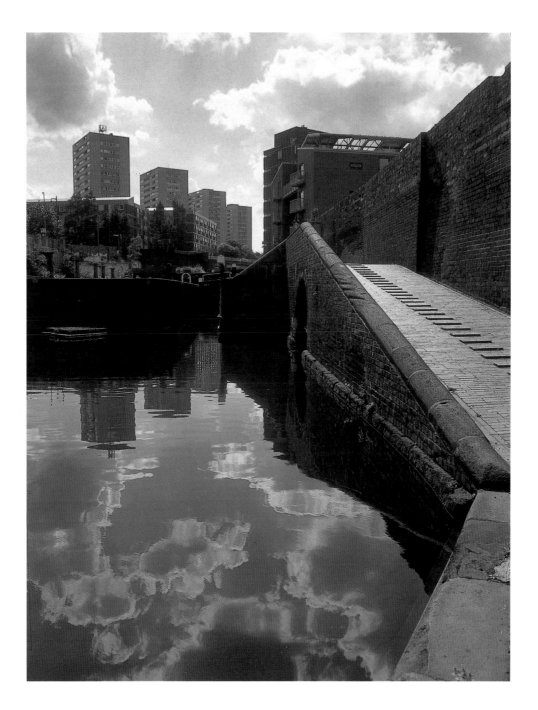

Looking up from Lock No.7 to Saturday Bridge. On the right is the side bridge that was the original entrance to an arm that served factories in Charlotte Street.

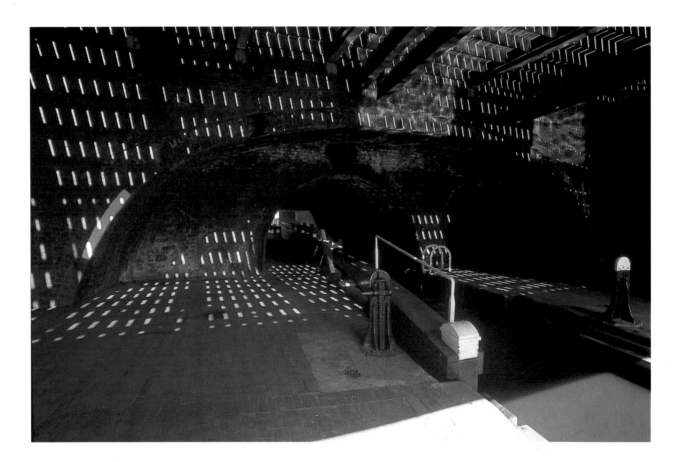

Lock No.9 under Newhall Street. The pedestrian boardwalk throws a dramatic shadow across the canal and entrance to the Newhall Street tunnel. This is also the access point from the canal to another of Birmingham's historic gems, the Jewellery Quarter.

From here the Birmingham & Fazeley Canal travels down to the junction at Aston, then under Spaghetti Junction under the M6 where it joins the Tame Valley Canal and out through the suburbs of Birmingham towards Tamworth.

In sharp contrast to the industrialised centre of the city the Birmingham & Fazeley Canal approaches the outskirts of Tamworth, and its junction with the Coventry Canal, and passes through Kingsbury. At Curdworth Bottom Lock is the distinctive Kingsbury swivel bridge.

Curdworth Bottom Lock and cottages are located in the heart of the Warwickshire countryside and situated alongside the Birmingham & Fazeley Canal, with access from the towpath, is Kingsbury Water Park. Landscaped from 620 acres of quarry the Park now has 30 pools and lakes and provides a mixture of wildlife, recreation and water sports. Running through the Park is part of the Heart of England Way footpath, which joins the towpath at these cottages and follows the canal up to Fisher's Mill Bridge, which leads to the 13th century Middleton Hall.

One of the many attractions of canals, particularly in rural locations is the canal side pub. You'll find the Dog and Doublet off Bodymoor Heath Lane alongside Cheadles Farm Bridge and lock.

Originally canal side pubs were the watering holes of the boat people who worked the canals and many of them have historical associations with this community of workers.

Today they are experiencing a new lease of life with boater and visitors alike. Many, like the Dog and Doublet provide good value food, in historical surroundings together with a very sociable stop for overnight mooring for boaters.

BIRMINGHAM & FAZELEY CANAL

In February 2001 Foot and Mouth Disease struck the North of England. Over the following months it spread virtually nationwide, devastating the farming community and changing the landscape overnight. Over 6 million animals were slaughtered in the attempt to contain and stop the disease. Subsequently, all access to towpaths was closed and for nearly 6 months nothing moved on the canal.

Fortunately, Cheadles Farm, alongside the Birmingham & Fazeley was not affected and days after the closure restrictions were lifted the cows above took a well-earned drink from the canal, while we sat outside the Dog and Doublet opposite, also quenching our thirst.

BIRMINGHAM & FAZELEY CANAL

The view looking from Bodymoor Heath Lane Bridge to Cheadles Farm Bridge and lock. The narrow boat is one of the first to navigate the Birmingham & Fazeley Canal after the lifting of the Foot and Mouth closures.

One of the real pleasures of the canal network nowadays is walking them. Today the majority of the network has upgraded towpaths making for a very enjoyable experience. The scene above is also unmistakably English and you can almost hear the silence and peace and quiet.

CHAPTER FIVE

DUDLEY CANAL

A commission from Bruce Harding of the British Waterways Photo Library found my wife and me spending a weekend at a damp, Russell Newbury Rally at the Black Country Museum near Tipton.

Russell Newbury is a make of engine and the Rally was a gathering of enthusiasts and their boats to talk technicalities, peer into the engine rooms, polish and oil their engines and take part in workshops as well as have a social get-together. Being totally ignorant of anything mechanical I concentrated on the images that all these boats created against the backdrop of the Black Country Museum.

DUDLEY CANAL

The Black Country Museum has been created around the old Dudley Canal and the entrance to the Dudley Tunnel, which is 3154 yards long, and the Singing Cavern. The entrance to the tunnel above is the perfect example of a practical need being answered with a simple civil engineering solution and creating a perfectly balanced piece of architecture, namely combining a tunnel portal with the need to gain access to the canal from both sides. It also illustrates the bricklayers art to perfection. The tunnel is only one boat width and has no towpath, therefore boats originally had to be poled or legged through.

Bows and sterns, ropes, fenders, Roses and Castles and canal ware seen against the wall of the Bottle and Glass Inn. This pub, like the buildings in the Museum were moved from various parts of the Black Country to create and preserve the social and industrial heritage of the area.

The Bottle and Glass Inn originally came from Brierley Hill Road, Brookmoor and backed onto the Stourbridge Flight of 16 locks. It was first known as The Bush, but by the 1840's it had become the Bottle and Glass.

DUDLEY CANAL

Narrow boat Jupiter moored alongside Browns Bridge, next to the entrance of the arm that leads to lime kilns that date from 1842. This arm was originally half a mile long and joined the Old Main Line from Birmingham to Wolverhampton and was called Lord Ward's Arm.

The Black Country Museum was established in 1975 and the first buildings were constructed on the site in the following year. The area got its name from the smoke of thousands of furnaces and chimneys that polluted the air. The coal from the seam below the Black Country was known as the Staffordshire Thick Coal and in some cases was only feet below the surface. The extraction of vast quantities of this coal led to dramatic subsidence, in fact the branch of Lord Ward's Arm to the limekilns was created by subsistence.

View looking through Browns Bridge to the lifting bridge across Lord Ward's Arm. This bridge, which links the Boatdock and Ironworks, was originally built across the railway transhipment basins at Lloyds Proving House near Factory Junction in Tipton. The deck of the bridge can be raised and lowered with a small hand-winch. Huge weights hanging on chains over the four pulleys balance the weight of the roadway, making it easier for vehicles to cross the canal.

There are three canals in the Dudley area; Dudley Number 1, Dudley Number 2 and the Stourbridge Canal. Dudley Number 1, starts at the Dudley Tunnel and was completed in 1792. Dudley Number 2 was built in 1798 and joins the Number 1 at the junction of Park Head. In 1846 the Dudley Canal Company merged with Birmingham Canal Navigations.

Moored opposite the Bottle and Glass Inn these narrow boats, all powered by Russell Newbury engines, demonstrate the subtle differences in design and construction and decoration that is a hallmark of canal narrow boats and feature the art of the rope fender maker.

DUDLEY CANAL

The Dudley Canals were originally part of the network of waterways linking the prosperous industrialised towns of the Black Country with Birmingham, London and the North. During the industrial revolution there were over 200 miles of canals in the area, today 130 miles still remain navigable and there are still many examples of the structures built by the pioneering engineers of the day. Many of these structures and buildings are now listed or scheduled ancient monuments, so they are thankfully protected for future generations to enjoy.

A view looking through the loading gauge that checked the height of boats before they entered into Dudley Tunnel, across the canal to the Trap Works.

Although it is shorter than the original building, Sidebothams Trap Works is a restored example of a typical small factory, with its distinctive barrel roof, to be found in the Black Country. It was moved to the Museum from Wednesfield near Wolverhampton and features many of the original machines used to manufacture traps. They were exported to many parts of the world from Wednesfield, which became a major centre for trap making.

CHAPTER SIX

WORCESTER & BIRMINGHAM CANAL

Tardebigge Top Lock on the Worcester and Birmingham Canal is the first lock for 14 miles from the beginning of the canal at Worcester Bar in Gas Street Basin in the heart of Birmingham. Construction of this first section of the canal was begun in 1792 and reached Tardebigge at the end of March 1807.

In the distance is the spire of St. Bartholomews Church. This tower and spire was constructed in 1777 replacing an earlier tower, which collapsed in 1775.

The lock keeper's cottage is unusual as it originally had the local bakery in its outbuildings.

Top Lock, No 58 at Tardebigge is one of the deepest narrow locks in the country, at 14 feet, because John Woodhouse the engineer for the Worcester and Birmingham in 1809 originally envisaged a system of boat lifts to reduce the number of locks.

However, Woodhouse's experimental boat lift was short-lived and was dismantled by John Rennie during reconstruction due to doubts that it would not stand the rough treatment by boatmen.

Because the lock was so deep there was also a side pound built in the garden of the lock cottage to save part of each lockful of water. The paddle stand can still be seen.

WORCESTER & BIRMINGHAM CANAL

Bridge No 56 looking from the Top Lock at Tardebigge. The Worcester and Birmingham Canal Bill was passed in 1791, but it was fiercely opposed by the Staffordshire and Worcestershire Canal Company fearing trade to the River Severn would be lost, resulting in the construction of the 7 foot transhipment bar at Gas Street Basin, preventing water from the Birmingham Canal Old Main Line reaching the Worcester and Birmingham.

Surveyed originally by John Snape and Josiah Clowes it was eventually opened throughout its 30 mile length in 1815.

The original pumping station for the Tardebigge flight is now a public house and restaurant. It was built to pump water up above the Top Lock from Tardebigge Reservoir and is located between the two.

Although the Worcester and Birmingham Canal carried a fair amount of traffic it was never as successful at linking Manchester and the North East via Birmingham with the West Cost via the River Severn as its promoters had hoped. Cargoes included coal and industrial goods to Worcester and agricultural produce was carried to Birmingham.

Cadburys first established a canal side factory before eventually moving to Bournville in 1879. Here they built a wharf and ran their own fleet of boats on the Worcester and Birmingham. This fleet was subsequently taken over and run by Severn and Canal Carrying Company. Cadburys however, stopped using the canal on a regular basis in 1961.

A distinctive feature of this section of the Worcester and Birmingham are the steps built into the lock at ground level to water level at the bottom. These are also built into Tardebigge Top Lock.

In the 1840's the railways in the area affected the Worcester and Birmingham Canal significantly with the effect of drastically reducing the tonnage carried on the canal. Then in 1874 it was purchased by Sharpness New Docks Company and became the Sharpness New Docks and Gloucester & Birmingham Navigation Company. Up until the 1900's the canal was busy, particularly with Severn & Canal Carrying Company boats, however this traffic then shrank.

Tardebigge Reservoir was constructed to supply and maintain water levels on the 30 locks of the Tardebigge Flight, including pumping water up to the Top Lock using the engine house. The reservoir therefore, because of its size, is a significant feature of the Worcester & Birmingham Canal and also provides an environment for both wildlife and birdlife, as well as an ideal picnic and countryside vantage point on its banks at its southern end.

WORCESTER & BIRMINGHAM CANAL

Over its entire length of 30 miles the Worcester & Birmingham Canal drops 453 feet and much of that is over the 30 locks at the Tardebigge Flight, which is the longest in England. During its commercial life this may have had an influence on the amount of traffic that used the canal, due to the time it must have taken to navigate this section.

Today, however, it has became one of the attractions of the canal and the view above, looking from the embankment of the Reservoir down the flight to Droitwich aerials and the Malverns in the distance, captures the beauty of the surrounding Worcestershire countryside.

CHAPTER SEVEN

GRAND UNION CANAL

Hatton Bottom Lock and cottage on the Grand Union Canal. Today the Grand Union is a network of 300 miles of canal, linking Leicester via the River Soar with Birmingham and down to London and the River Thames at Brentford and at Limehouse Docks, via the Regents Canal. It was formed in 1929 by merging 8 canals and creating a direct link between the capital and the heart of the Midlands.

The lock cottage opposite Bottom Lock No. 26 is a classic piece of canal architecture, with its white pointed brickwork, elegant lines, tall chimneys and outbuildings. It makes a picture postcard scene, even though it's sandwiched between the busy A46 Warwick bypass, and the Leamington to Birmingham railway line.

Hatton Bottom Lock from under the bridge of the A46 and looking towards Hatton. Behind the camera past the bridge is Budbrooke Junction and the Saltisford Arm. This was where the original Warwick & Birmingham met the Warwick and Napton Canal on the outskirts of Warwick town. All that now remains of the ½ mile Saltisford Arm that was rescued from dereliction between 1982 and 1988 is now managed by the Saltisford Canal Trust.

A view of Lock 42 outside the British Waterways Hatton Offices.

During its heyday it was a thriving maintenance yard, known as Hatton Shops, where lock gates were built as well as general repairs carried out. Alongside the canal was a crane and the yard had its own blacksmiths, while just above Lock 43 there is a dry dock, which is still used today.

The distinctive paddle gear, which encloses and protects the mechanism, is a feature of the Grand Union Canal and the tall building with large windows is a landmark at Hatton, originally being an office and used rather like a railway signal box, affording a view up and down the Hatton Flight.

Of the eight canals that formed the Grand Union in 1929 two that now form part of the system began in Birmingham. The Warwick and Birmingham Act of Parliament was authorised in March 1793 and joined the Digbeth Branch of the Birmingham Canal Navigations. Its terminus was on the outskirts of Warwick at Saltisford Basin, 22 miles from Birmingham, and was finally opened in March 1800.

The Birmingham and Warwick Junction Canal was completed in 1844 and joined the Birmingham and Fazeley at Salford Junction with the Warwick and Birmingham Canal at Camp Hill Locks, near Bordesley Junction.

The restored Hatton Maintenance Depot is now the home of the British Waterways Heritage Skills Centre. The new building to the left of the tall office is a stonemason's centre and behind in restored buildings is the blacksmith's forge. At this centre British Waterways now offer, for both BW staff and independent organisations, the opportunity to be trained in traditional building skills, such as stone masonry, lime mortar pointing, bricklaying and blacksmithing.

The restoration of the former depot has successfully retained the character of the original buildings as well as incorporating new additions.

Between Lock 42 and the figure by the building can be seen the original narrow lock. The new locks that were widened in 1932 now allow pairs of boats, as well as broad beamed craft, to use the lock, therefore saving time and water.

Hatton offices from across the reservoir that provides water for the 21 Flight of Hatton Locks. Out of shot to the right, is Hatton Bridge, rebuilt in concrete in the 1930's, which is also a turnover bridge, moving the towpath to the north bank.

To the left is Lock 42, which is the beginning of a group of six locks in quick succession, which was known by canal folk as 'the thick'. Halfway down the Hatton Flight is bridge 52 which was also rebuilt in the 1930's out of concrete and is now known as Ugly Bridge.

Early morning mist over Lock 46 – Hatton Top Lock. Access to the lock keeper's cottage is via the wooden bridge in front of the lock.

On 30 October 1934 the Duke of Kent carried out the official opening of the new locks at this point. The widening programme started in 1932 to improve Knowle, Hatton and Stockton flights from narrow single to wide locks.

A classic view of Hatton locks looking down from Lock 42 towards Warwick with the tower of St. Mary's Church in the distance. The 21 locks that make up the Hatton Flight are known as the 'Stairway to Heaven' and drop the canal 146½ feet down to Warwick in just under 2½ miles.

In the distance is Middle Lock Bridge and alongside this is the site of Asylum Wharf. This is where coal was off loaded from the working boats by patients of the Hatton Mental Asylum, for the hospital boilers. The Asylum was virtually self-contained, including a farm and a theatre. Today the original main buildings have been developed into luxury apartments and new housing has been built in the grounds.

Knowle locks looking towards Warwick. When widening began in 1932 they were reduced from 6 narrow to 5 wide locks, each with a drop of 8' 4½". In order to maintain water levels a reservoir was incorporated with a pumping station, at the bottom lock which lifts water back to the summit.

As well as paddle gear, this section of the Grand Union Canal also features a distinctive painting style applied to the white ends of the lock beams.

The total drop over the length of the five locks at Knowle is a dramatic 42 feet over a very short distance. They are also only 100 yards apart, so side pounds have been provided to maintain sufficient capacities without major fluctuations to the water levels. These side pounds have been incorporated where the old narrow locks were built, alongside the towpath and now also provide a natural habitat for wildfowl and plants.

In the view above the uncompromising shape of the 1930's concrete lock is in sharp contrast to the usual engineering blue and red brick of many of the restored canals in the Heart of England.

GRAND UNION CANAL

As the sun sets, the locks at Knowle appear to be floating on water.

After the acquisition of the Warwick & Birmingham and the Birmingham & Warwick Junction Canals by the Regents Canal Company, to form the Grand Union in 1929, the modernisation programme to widen all the narrow locks to enable broad beamed 70 ton barges to navigate between London and Birmingham was begun. However, Knowle was the furthest point north that the locks were modernised. Initially this helped the Grand Union to compete with the roads and the railways, but the company's failure to widen the locks all the way to the centre of Birmingham may have been a factor in the decline of trade on the canal.

GRAND UNION CANAL

A cold and frosty morning at Kingswood Junction, Lapworth, where the Grand Union is linked to the Stratford-upon-Avon Canal. The present link was completed in 1995, but as far back as 1802 a short branch canal existed to link the two.

In the view above is one of the distinctive split bridges that are a feature of the southern section of the Stratford-upon-Avon Canal. This allowed the rope from horse drawn boats to pass through the gap in the centre, therefore saving time. The two bridge sections are made of iron and cantilevered from brick piers. The man crossing the bridge was an angler who was looking for a possible spot to fish, even with ice on the water. And I thought I was mad.

CHAPTER EIGHT

OXFORD CANAL

The Oxford Canal begins at its junction with the Coventry Canal at Hawkesbury (see page 15) and runs for 77 miles to the historic city of Oxford. It gently winds its way south travelling through Rugby and Banbury to Oxford where it meets the River Thames. The Grand Union Canal joins it at Napton and they share the same channel until Braunston Turn where the Grand Union heads south via Milton Keynes and Watford to London.

At Lower Shuckburgh, 1½ miles from the junction at Napton, a hire boat heads south passing under footbridge No 105. The boat is one of the Rose Narrowboat fleet from Stretton-under-Fosse near Brinklow. In the distance is the parish church of St. John the Baptist.

At Braunston the Oxford and Grand Union Canals meet. Looking across the Horseley Iron Works bridge the former Toll Office, called Stop House, is now the offices of British Waterways. Originally monies were collected here from boats passing between the Oxford Canal and Grand Union Canal. The bridge spans the entrance into the busy marina, which has a number of boat builders and businesses, as well as residential housing. In its commercial heyday many of the well known carrying companies were based here, including Barlows, Fellows, Morton & Clayton and Pickfords.

OXFORD CANAL

The Oxford Canal was constructed 10 years before the Grand Union, forming part of the network of inland waterways linking the industrialised Midlands with London via the Thames.

Engineered by James Brindley (1716-1772), it received the Royal Assent in April 1769 and construction began in September of that year at Hawkesbury. Brindley believed in following the natural contours of the land to avoid expensive construction of tunnels and aqueducts.

Early morning, the canal meanders peacefully around the countryside near Fenny Compton at the beginning of a number of elaborate curves to Napton. The site of the medieval village of Wormleighton is in the distance on the right, while on the bend the residential moorings are located alongside Freckleton Spinney.

Like Birmingham and Coventry, Banbury has recently invested in the redevelopment of its centre incorporating the canal corridor. The Castle Quay Shopping Centre on the right has become a new focal point in the town. Also in the redevelopment is a new Museum, left, and the restoration of the historic Tooley's Boatyard which is under the bridge, to the right. Established in 1790 boats were built here to meet the need for narrow boats for the Oxford, which was the first

narrow canal to be constructed. They were built and launched sideways up until the 1920's and repairs were carried out in the dry dock, the oldest on the Oxford Canal.

Beyond this bridge is Factory Street Lift Bridge, the first of a number of distinctive wooden bridges, which are a feature of the southern section of the Oxford Canal.

OXFORD CANAL

South of Banbury the route of the Oxford Canal becomes less meandering as it passes through the rural Oxfordshire countryside, following, and in some places running alongside, the course of the River Cherwell.

At Kings Sutton, looking north to Grants Lock is bridge N.176, Bushy Furze Lift Bridge. Also running parallel with the Oxford Canal at this point, and crossing it beyond Grants Lock in the distance, is the M40 motorway which creates the constant drone of traffic noise across the landscape. However, on the day I shot this section there had been a major accident and the motorway was at a standstill. Silence reigned and for a short while the Oxford became one the most peaceful canals in the country again.

Although the canal was very busy for the first 35 years the opening of the Grand Junction in 1805 and the arrival of the railways in the l840's signalled the beginning of a loss of traffic on the southern section of the Oxford, although it remained commercially viable for another 100 years.

The Church of Holy Cross at Shipton-on-Cherwell looks down on the Oxford Canal at a section known as Thrupp Wide. Beyond the bend on which the Church is located, between bridges 220 and 219 is Shipton-on-Cherwell Railway Bridge. Here on Christmas Eve 1874 a tragic railway accident occurred when nine carriages fell from the bridge, onto the frozen canal, killing 34 people. Just past this bridge, between Shipton

Weir Lock and Bates Lock, the River Cherwell and the Oxford Canal become one.

By the 1950's commercial traffic all but disappeared and the South Oxford, like many canals during this period was threatened with closure, however it was saved after considerable public pressure.

OXFORD CANAL

Financial problems delayed the work on the Oxford Canal but it eventually reached the City of Oxford in 1789 and was officially opened on New Years Day 1790.

Looking towards Oxford city centre the canal joins the River Thames, beyond Isis Lock and is crossed by the elegant Isis iron bridge. The canal also runs to the left of the bridge 200 yards to Hythe Bridge and its terminus. Originally the canal ended further south, where Nuffield College now stands, at Worcester Street Wharf and New Road Coal Wharf.

Isis Lock provides access to the Thames via Sheepwash Channel and it was built to allow larger Thames barges access to the Oxford Canal Companies wharves and link the waterway with Liverpool and London, bringing prosperity to the City of Oxford.

BIOGRAPHY

Alan Tyers was born in Coventry in 1944 and was selected to join the College of Art, at the age of 13, and trained to be a fine artist.

At the age of eighteen he left to pursue a career in advertising and design. At that time his interest in photography began and was encouraged by his friend Derek Watkins, a leading photographic magazine journalist, photographer and author of several books on the subject.

During the course of his career photography took a back seat however until in 1991 he started his own creative consultancy. As part of the services he offered, he developed his photographic skills, seeing images from the eye of an art director and designer.

His clients include the Royal Agricultural Society of England, City Development Directorate Coventry, Rare Breeds Survival Trust, several British Waterways offices and he is a selected photographer for the British Waterways Photographic library. He is also represented by Collections in London.

He lives in Leamington Spa, Warwickshire.

ACKNOWLEDGMENTS

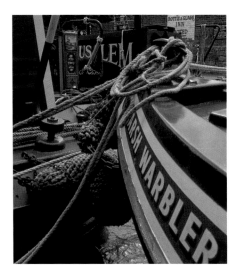 

I would like to thank the many people who have helped me, not only in the production of this book, but also during my assignments and those who have taken an interest in my work and provided valuable advice and encouragement. I'd particularly like to thank Annette Simpson at British Waterways Lapworth, who started it all off with my first commission and Edward Moss, also at Lapworth for his help and enthusiasm, particularly during my research. Also Lorraine Smith, Edgbaston and Lucie Unstead at Branston. A big thank you to Lucie Hancock at British Waterways Fradley, for all her support, encouragement and knowledge, and Bruce Harding of British Waterways Photo Library Watford, for his help and for sending me to so many interesting locations. To Alan Brewin my publisher for his enthusiasm and support and Alistair Brewin for his help in the design and production of this, my first book. Finally, my wife Lyn, for all her support, encouragement, patience and understanding, especially when assisting me on location and typing all the captions.